A Note to

Eyewitness Readers is a compelling new program for beginning readers, designed in conjunction with leading literacy experts, including Dr. Linda Gambrell, President of the National Reading Conference and past board member of the International Reading Association.

Eyewitness has become the most trusted name in illustrated books, and this new series combines the highly visual *Eyewitness* approach with engaging, easy-to-read stories. Each *Eyewitness Reader* is guaranteed to capture a child's interest while developing his or her reading skills, general knowledge, and love of reading.

The four levels of *Eyewitness Readers* are aimed at different reading abilities, enabling you to choose the books that are exactly right for your children:

Level 1, for Preschool to Grade 1
Level 2, for Grades 1 to 3
Level 3, for Grades 2 and 3
Level 4, for Grades 2 to 4

The "normal" age at which a child begins to read can be anywhere from three to eight years old, so these levels are intended only as a general guideline.

No matter which level you select, you can be sure that you are helping your child learn to read, then read to learn!

A DK PUBLISHING BOOK
www.dk.com

Project Editor Louise Pritchard
Art Editor Jill Plank

Senior Editor Linda Esposito
Senior Art Editor
Diane Thistlethwaite
US Editor Regina Kahney
Production Melanie Dowland
Picture Researcher Andrea Sadler
Illustrator Peter Dennis
Space Consultant Carole Stott
Indexer Lynn Bresler

Reading Consultant
Linda Gambrell

First American Edition, 2000
2 4 6 8 10 9 7 5 3 1
Published in the United States by DK Publishing, Inc.
95 Madison Avenue, New York, New York 10016

Published in Great Britain by Dorling Kindersley Limited.

Eyewitness Readers™ is a trademark of
Dorling Kindersley Limited, London.

Library of Congress Cataloging-in-Publication Data
Hayden, Kate.
    Astronaut: living in space / by Kate Hayden. – 1st American ed.
    p. cm. – (Dorling Kindersley readers)
    Summary: Describes the various steps necessary for an astronaut to
prepare for a flight into space and follows astronaut Linda Gardner
as she trains for her space shuttle mission.
    ISBN 0-7894-5422-X (hc) – ISBN 0-7894-5421-1 (pb)
    1. Life support systems (Space environment)–Juvenile literature.
    2. Astronauts–juvenile literature. [1. Astronauts.] I. Title. II. Series.
    III. Eyewitness readers. Level 2.

TL1500 .H39 2000
629.47'7–dc21.   99-044159

Color reproduction by Colourscan, Singapore
Printed and bound in Belgium by Proost

The publisher would like to thank the following
for their kind permission to reproduce their photographs:
c=center; b=bottom; l=left; r=right; t=top

Genesis Space Photo Library: 14cr; N.A.S.A.: 10cl; **Planet Earth Pictures**:
4br, 15t, 30–31; **Popperfoto**: Reuters 12br; **Science Photo Library**:
A. Sokolov & A. Leonov/ASAP 20bl; **NASA**: 6, 11, 13, 21, 23, 26cl;
Times Syndication: 7br.

DK EYEWITNESS READERS

Level **2** GRADES 1-3

Astronaut
Living in Space

Written by Kate Hayden

DK

DK PUBLISHING, INC.

Linda is an astronaut
on the space shuttle.
She is going to repair
a broken telescope.
Linda loves going into space.
It is very exciting.
As she looks out the window
she can see Earth below.
What a view!
She can see towns
and rivers and mountains.

Telescopes
We can look at the stars
and planets through
telescopes on Earth.
But we can see even farther
through telescopes in space.

Linda had wanted
to go into space
since she was
a little girl.

When she applied for
a job as an astronaut,
thousands of other people
applied, too.
But only six people
would get in.

Linda had to take a lot of tests.
Doctors checked her heart,
lungs, eyes, and ears.
Finally she got the job.

Science in space
Many astronauts are scientists.
Doctors study what happens
to our bodies in space.
Biologists study what happens
to plants and animals.

Linda spent 18 months
training to be an astronaut.
During her training,
she went on a machine
that let her move
as if she were
in space.

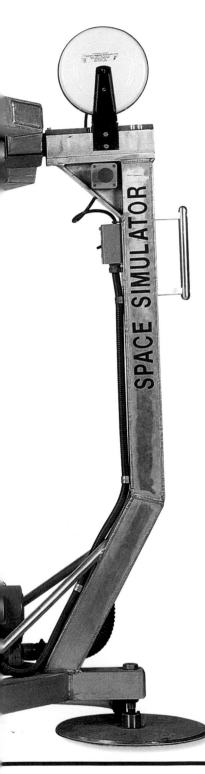

Space is very
different from Earth.
On Earth,
a force called gravity
keeps everyone
on the ground.
In space, there is
less gravity.
Astronauts can
float around.
This is called
being weightless.
It happens
because of
the way the shuttle
moves around Earth.

SPACE SIMULATOR

Before each mission,
astronauts train for the job
they will do in space.
For this mission, Linda learned
how to repair a telescope.

She practiced
on a model
of a telescope
in a swimming pool –
being underwater
is a bit like

being in space.
Linda practiced again and again
until she was perfect.
Then she was ready
to go up in the space shuttle.

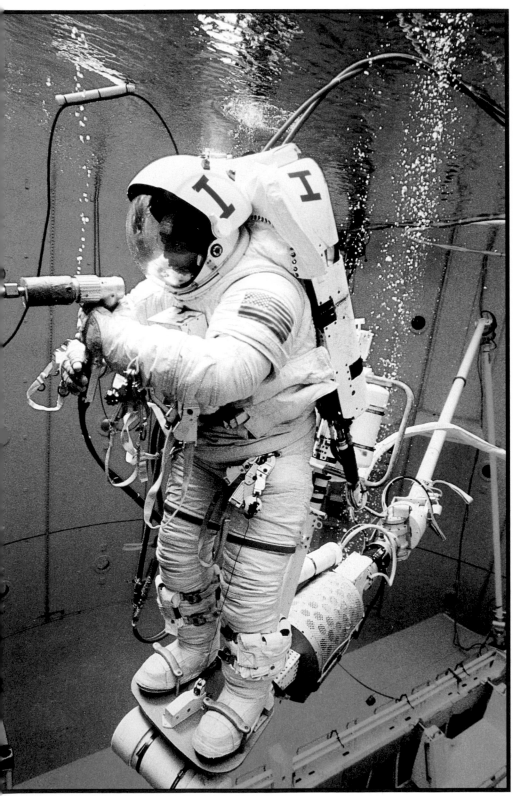

This is Linda's fourth mission.
Each time the astronauts
strap themselves into their seats
Linda gets butterflies.
The final countdown begins.
Ten, nine, eight, seven, six, five,
four, three, two, one, lift-off!
There is a deafening, thundering
ROOAAARRRR
as the rockets fire the shuttle
off the launch pad.

Space suit
Astronauts wear
special orange suits
for take-off and landing.
The suits help them to cope
with the unusual forces.

People at Launch Control on Earth
watch the take-off.
They can talk to the crew
at any time.

In just 30 seconds,
the shuttle leaves
the blue sky
and enters
the darkness
of space.
The rockets and fuel tank
drop away.
The rockets are collected
from the sea
to be used on
another mission.

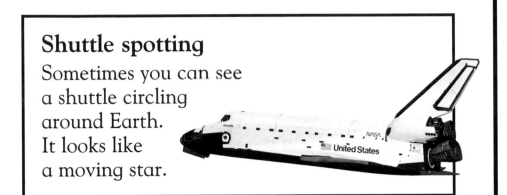

Shuttle spotting

Sometimes you can see
a shuttle circling
around Earth.
It looks like
a moving star.

Now Linda changes into trousers
and a T-shirt to relax.
She has pockets
for her pens and snacks.
Otherwise they will
float away.

15

The space shuttle
is made up of three parts –
a space plane called the orbiter,
a fuel tank, and two rockets.
The rockets fire the orbiter
into space.
The orbiter carries equipment,
such as a laboratory, or a telescope,
in the cargo bay.
The crew uses a robotic arm
to move things in and out of
the cargo bay.

There are eight astronauts
on Linda's mission.
They live and work in the cabin.
The mission commander is
in charge.
He sits with the pilot
at the orbiter's controls.

A few hours after take-off,
some of the crew take a break.
Linda joins them for lunch.
She straps herself into a seat.
The food is in packages
held on a tray.
Linda ties her tray to her knee.
She eats with a fork and spoon.
But she sucks her drink
out of a pack so the drops
don't float around.

Space food

There are more than
70 different
kinds of food available.
Some are ready-to-eat.
Others need water.

Finally they reach
the broken telescope.
Linda puts on a special suit
for walking out in space.
It has oxygen to breathe
because there is no air in space.
It also has headphones
and a microphone in the helmet
so Linda can talk to the crew.
A jet-propelled backpack
helps Linda move around.

Space walk

Russian astronaut
Alexei Leonov was
the first person
to walk in space,
in March 1965.

Out in space at last!
Linda begins to repair
the telescope.
But the telescope is bent
and her repair tool does not fit.
This means she must
get the telescope
into the cargo bay
to do the repairs.
Linda tells the commander
about her problem.
He moves out the robotic arm
to pick up the telescope.
But will it reach?
Linda stands on the arm
and gives directions.

The arm is
just long enough.
Linda catches the telescope.
The commander brings it back
on the robotic arm
to the orbiter's cargo bay.

It takes a few hours
for Linda to repair the telescope.
Then she helps the commander
to put it back in space.
Linda is happy
that she has done her job.

Now Linda has to work out
on an exercise machine.
She is lighter in space
than on Earth,
so her bones and muscles
do not have to work very hard.
She must exercise
for two hours a day.
This stops her from growing weak.

Linda works hard
on the machine.
A doctor checks
her health
as she
exercises.

After her workout,
Linda washes with wet wipes.
There are no showers on board.
Drops of floating water
can damage the equipment.
There is a bathroom though.

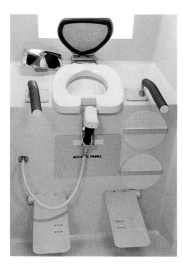 It sucks everything
safely away.

Soon it is
Linda's turn to sleep.
She climbs into
a bunk in the wall and lies down.
The astronauts sleep in shifts,
so some of the crew members
are always awake to work.

It is time to return to Earth!
This could be dangerous.
Earth is surrounded by
a blanket of gases
called the atmosphere.
The orbiter must reenter
the atmosphere at
the perfect angle.
If it reenters
too steeply, it will burn up.
If it comes down
at too shallow an angle,
it will bounce into space.
The pilot gets it just right.
The orbiter reenters
the atmosphere safely.

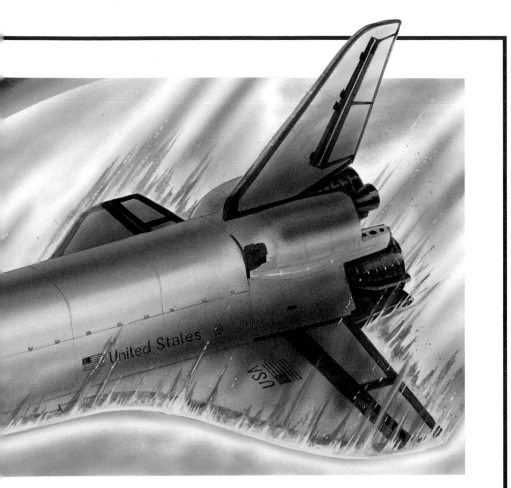

Linda looks out the window.
The orbiter is red-hot – it is 2,500°F.
But it is covered with
special tiles to stop it
from burning up.
Suddenly, a tile
flies past the window.

Linda does not worry.
There are still enough tiles
on the orbiter to protect it.
The orbiter starts to glide
through the air.

In only 14 seconds
the space craft will
touch down.
The pilot lowers
the landing gear.

Then the orbiter lands.
A drag chute, like a parachute,
helps to slow it down.

The astronauts have to wait for
the orbiter to cool down.
At last they come out.
Linda looks up into space.
She is already looking forward
to another mission.

Space facts

In space, astronauts are up to
three-quarters of an inch taller
than they are on Earth.

The heart does not
need to pump as hard
in space as it does on Earth,
so it can get weak.

The astronauts in a space shuttle
use up oxygen all the time,
so fresh oxygen is circulated
around the craft.

Water vapor from astronauts'
breath is collected
and recycled for drinking.

If an astronaut needs to shave,
he must vacuum up the cuttings
before they float away.

People in space can keep in touch
with their family and friends
using a laptop computer.

A woodpecker once delayed the
launch of the space shuttle. It
pecked more than 75 holes in the
casing around the fuel tank.

The first creature to be born
in space was a quail chick.